Other Books by David A. Anderson

Letters Across the Divide, coauthored with
   Brent Zuercher
Multicultural Ministry
Gracism: The Art of Inclusion
Multicultural Ministry Handbook, coedited with
   Margarita R. Cabellon

I Forgrace You

Doing Good to Those Who Have Hurt You

Dr. David A. Anderson

IVP Books

An imprint of InterVarsity Press
Downers Grove, Illinois

InterVarsity Press
P.O. Box 1400, Downers Grove, IL 60515-1426
World Wide Web: www.ivpress.com
E-mail: email@ivpress.com

*InterVarsity Press®️ is the book-publishing division of InterVarsity Christian
Fellowship/USA®️, a movement of students and faculty active on campus at hundreds
of universities, colleges and schools of nursing in the United States of America, and a
member movement of the International Fellowship of Evangelical Students. For
information about local and regional activities, write Public Relations Dept.,
InterVarsity Christian Fellowship/USA, 6400 Schroeder Rd., P.O. Box 7895, Madison,
WI 53707-7895, or visit the IVCF website at <www.intervarsity.org>.*

*All Scripture quotations, unless otherwise indicated, are taken from the Holy Bible,
New International Version®️. NIV®️. Copyright ©1973, 1978, 1984 by International
Bible Society. Used by permission of Zondervan Publishing House. All rights reserved.*

*While all stories in this book are true, some names and identifying information in this
book have been changed to protect the privacy of the individuals involved.*

Design: Cindy Kiple
Images: orange tulip: hermi/iStockphoto
*   large crack: ©Sam Woolford/iStockphoto*

ISBN 978-0-8308-3828-8

Printed in the United States of America ∞

Library of Congress Cataloging-in-Publication Data

Anderson, David A., 1966-
  *I forgrace you: doing good to those who have hurt you / David A.
Anderson.*
     p. cm.
  Includes bibliographical references.
  ISBN 978-0-8308-3828-8 (pbk.: alk. paper)
  *1. Forgiveness—Religious aspects—Christianity. 2. Grace
(Theology) I. Title.*
  BV4647.F55A63 2010
  241′.4—dc22

                                                      2010052961

P	15	14	13	12	11	10	9	8	7	6	5	4	3	2	1
Y	23	22	21	20	19	18	17	16	15	14	13	12	11		

To my beloved mother, Icie Anderson Jackson:

You have been the epitome of forgiveness and grace in my life. I dedicate this book to you.

To my beloved wife, Amber:

Thank you for your forgraceness in my life and in our marriage. I love you.

To my beloved daughter, Asia:

May the grace of your mother and grandmother be passed on to and through you to the next generation.

Contents

Introduction

I Forgrace You is intended to free you. This book will empower you to let go of hurts and forgive those who have injured you. In time you will be able to bless them. Yes, I said bless them.

The idea of blessing the one who has injured you might make you want to throw this book across the room. You may have resolved in your heart to never be kind to the person who damaged you. In fact, maybe your only desire is to throw the book at them! Don't do it. There is a better way. Going this way is redemptive in nature, spiritual in essence, practical in application and healing in its effect.

I call this *forgraceness*—the powerful union of forgiveness married to grace. This concept is not my own; it originated from the heart of Jesus

Christ. He spoke it into existence with the wisdom that comes from heaven. Jesus said that he has come to set us free, and those he sets free are "free indeed" (John 8:36)

Living by forgraceness will give you the strength and grace to live another day, another decade, a lifetime. How can I promise such a result? Because when applied, forgraceness will free you from the graceless weight of guilt, shame, anger, bitterness, contempt and the undue pressure of unforgiveness.

In order for the claim of strength and grace to become a reality, allowing you to live another day (or decade), you must commit to what this book teaches and be open to what God may be saying to you as you prayerfully meditate on this concept. When I say *live*, I don't mean adding to the quantity of your years. I mean the kind of living that Jesus Christ promises to those who follow him. Jesus said, "I have come that you may have life, and have it to the full" (John 10:10).

The life Jesus offers is not free of pain, hurt, disappointment and trial. But it will allow you to breathe in hope and exhale possibility. Jesus promises quality, eternal life and deep spiritual meaning. When we place our faith in him as the ultimate grace giver and forgiver, Jesus gives us the grace to hold on to him through the darkest times. You can and will prevail over your circumstances, even if they have paralyzed you more than anyone can imagine.

When I told my wife, Amber, that I wanted to write a book called *I Forgrace You*, she immediately responded, "But I'm not ready to forgive some people yet!" We both laughed at her reaction. I assured her that no one would be forcing her to forgive, but I sure would like her to let me off the hook for a few things!

Forgraceness is not simply about letting people off the hook. You will discover, however, that *you* will be the one let off the hook as you apply this precious rule of freedom. While Amber's reaction was a bit defensive (and a bit tongue-in-cheek), I assured her that we all need grace to make it through life, and that none of us could live without generous doses of God's grace and his Spirit's power. As you read this book, you will need much grace too. It takes grace to forgive.

How to Use This Book

Let me explain how I want you to use this book. First, prayerfully read it and digest the spiritually and emotionally powerful principles of grace and forgiveness packed within. Second, please give it away! That's right—pass on to others the beautiful gift of God's forgraceness. At the end of the book is a page for you to share with your recipient why you are giving it to him or her.

Now, though, let's journey toward God's design for our freedom.

I

Forgiveness Is Golden

I once heard a story of a woman who had nine and a half fingers. I'll call her Margaret. She was angry, often frowning, and typically on edge whenever she interacted with others. People in her sphere of influence would not have a problem calling her a b**ch. Not to her face of course, but even the holiest of folks thought it.

Margaret, a wrinkled fifty-five-year-old woman who looked like she was in her late seventies, with gray hair, wrinkled cheeks and a naturally depressive face when not smiling, peered into the mirror one morning for a few extra seconds before rushing out to her routine job of customer service (go figure!) at the local home improvement superstore. Almost paralyzed by the face that haunted her as she gazed into the mirror, Margaret was confronted with the fact that she hated what she had become—older, angrier, crankier—and it showed on the stress lines of her soured face. So Margaret resolved to cross the threshold of a counselor's office door for an attempt at therapy.

In her first session Margaret told the counselor that she was angry and didn't know why. She admitted that her attitude had aged her significantly and that she was unhappy with her life. After the counselor listened for a while, he inadvertently touched on a sensitive subject when he asked Margaret about her half finger. "How did that happen?" he asked.

Margaret spent the next thirty minutes describing how her sister accidentally chopped off the tip of her finger when they were little girls. Playing house at the kitchen table, things got out of hand as they were chopping onions. One missed chop had everyone screaming. The shock was so great that the pain is not memorable.

"Before I knew it," Margaret explained, "almost half of my finger was missing and irreparable. Growing up, can you imagine the looks I have received? The laughter from kids in school and the feelings of being a freak?"

After listening some more, the counselor asked the million-dollar question, "Have you forgiven your sister?"

"No," Margaret responded curtly.

"It's been four decades now, Margaret. When do you suspect you will forgive your sister?"

With her eyes becoming bloodshot, Margaret lifted her disfigured hand to the counselor's face, leaned forward and retorted, "When the finger comes back!"

We all know how ridiculous Margaret's answer was, but her anger and unforgiveness were so deep that she was basically saying, "Just as the finger will not return, I will never forgive my sister."

How does our resolve to not forgive grow so strong? Anger, which often comes from hurt, nursed over time eventually forms into a root of bitterness that is difficult to unearth. It dwells with us for years and becomes normal, part of our emotional fabric. Such bitterness eats away at our joy and leaves us as aged and angry as Margaret.

Like Margaret's finger, there are some things that we have lost that will never come back. Holding on to the anger and remaining mad at the person who hurt us, whether intentionally or unintentionally, is not going to bring back what we lost, but it will add to what we have lost and steal more away from us.

If unintentional pain from others is hard to bear, those who have purposed to hurt, abuse, betray or destroy us may seem impossible to endure. I'm sure that Margaret's sister didn't mean to hurt her. The accidental dismembering of Margaret's finger must have weighed on her conscience all of her growing-up years. But what could she do about it? Margaret's sister would love to hear the words "I forgive you" from her sister. If the circumstances were reversed, wouldn't Margaret want forgiveness? Of course. Therefore Margaret's counselor tried to convince her to forgive using the golden rule.

The Golden Rule

Everyone knows the golden rule. It's the old adage "Do to others as you would have them do to you" (Luke 6:31). Jesus teaches us that we are to treat one another the way we want to be treated, and thus we can minimize hurting one another.

In application, this rule says, "I will be nice to you because that is the way I want you to treat me." It says, "I will forgive you because I want to be forgiven when I make a mistake." To forgive in this manner is one thing, but what about forgiving those who don't have your friendship? Whether forgiving a friend, a relative or an enemy, forgiveness can be difficult. Even though it can be challenging, forgiveness is golden because it is expected and is good.

Forgiveness is God's pathway to redemption for human beings. He forgives all who ask, because his Son, Jesus, has paid the penalty of human transgressions, which places us in right standing with God. We accept the gift of salvation by faith. It is a free gift offered to all who will accept it.

However, forgiveness is not always accepted, is it? Just like many will not accept the free gift of God's forgiveness, some won't accept your forgiveness either. But that is not the point. You must offer forgiveness regardless of the response of the recipient. Whether your forgiveness is accepted by the recipient is his or her issue. The real question is this: Will you forgive?

Personal Forgiveness in Our Marriage

Amber and I have lived what I'm writing about. Over the years we have struggled to keep our marriage happy and healthy. After more than two decades together I would be lying if I did not admit that we have hurt one another deeply at times. I can also testify to the grace of the Lord through many of our darkest hours, and sometimes years.

I will never forget the day I confessed significant personal transgressions to Amber and admitted to sins I was ashamed of and had kept in secret. Her forgiveness seemed impossible to conceive. I wasn't even sure I wanted her forgiveness, because I knew I didn't deserve it. Over time and with a lot

of work we were able to trudge through the difficulties of our past, both mine and hers.

I once again tasted the passionate fruit of her forgiveness and grace. I am not saying that forgiveness
is easy, but it is necessary. Forgiveness does not
promise that marriages will endure and all homes
will be happy, but it does promise to release us from
the multiplying effects of negativity and bitterness
that darken the soul and depress the mind.

What Does It Mean to Forgive?

Forgiveness means to release people from retaliation and revenge. It is setting them free from the
prison of our unforgiving heart and not holding
against them what they did to us.

The act of forgiveness is both a choice and a
process. The choice to forgive must be made repeatedly, and then reaffirmed every time our
emotions cause us to want to strangle afresh those
who hurt us.

When we forgive, we are letting the other person go. We are releasing him or her to God's judgment and trusting that God knows how to deal
with the person and his or her sin.

Forgiveness Is Not Reconciliation

In order for two to walk together there must be

agreement. In order for reconciliation to take place, two people or groups of people must sit down and make peace. It is important to know that while reconciliation takes two people working toward agreement, forgiveness only takes one person. One can forgive another whether an apology is made or not. No agreement is needed. The other party doesn't even need to know that we are forgiving them when we do it.

While I believe in, preach about and promote reconciliation, this is not a book about reconciliation. I have already written books on that topic: *Letters Across the Divide* (2001), *Multicultural Ministry* (2004) and *Gracism* (2007). It is extremely important for people and cultures to reconcile, but you need to know that the first step in reconciliation is forgiveness.

Before Jesus could reconcile with us, he had to first forgive us. This is why Jesus said on the cross, "Father, forgive them, for they do not know what they are doing" (Luke 23:34).

Here is the big question, Can you forgive? Will you forgive even if you are not asked by the one who offended you? Can you say like Christ "Father, forgive them"? As hard as it is, it will lead to both your death, dying to yourself, and your resurrection, a new lease on life.

First Word and Last Act

After Jesus cried out, "Father, forgive them," he received much abuse from his accusers. While forgiveness was Jesus' first word on the cross, it was also his last act. On the cross Christ's final expression of ministry was to forgive the thief that was hanging next to him. This man likely lived in rebellion toward God and society. He was given the death sentence because of his criminal behavior.

Yet in his dying breath the thief asked Jesus to remember him when Jesus arrived at his heavenly home. This was the criminal's way of seeking forgiveness. Jesus didn't wait until arriving in heaven before extending eternal forgiveness to the thief. Jesus said, "Today you will be with me in paradise" (Luke 23:43).

Jesus' demonstration of redemption is our model as well. We must speak forgiveness, pray forgiveness and demonstrate forgiveness. Forgiveness is the way to new life. It is the way to freedom. Go ahead, ask God to forgive you and others. In doing so, you will live now and forevermore.

Back to the Half Finger

Margaret's lost half finger may never come back, but her joy might. Her peace, beauty, freedom and life could come back. But it will only begin to when she agrees with the counselor to do what she had been unwilling to do for decades. The counselor encouraged Margaret to release her sister from the prison of unforgiveness in her heart.

Margaret confessed that one of the reasons she had held on to her unforgiveness for so long was because of the constant reminder of what happened to her—nine and a half fingers. Margaret, like many of us, made the mistake of equating forgiveness with forgetting.

Margaret finally had a breakthrough when her counselor explained, "Margaret, you do know that forgiving doesn't mean forgetting, don't you?" Margaret said, "No. In fact, I will never forget."

"Margaret," the counselor softly stated, "scars can be a reminder of what you have endured. They can remind you of what you have forgiven. Your half finger has the possibility of no longer being a source of your anger but a memory of God's grace and how much progress you have made, even with the limits you have had to endure."

When Margaret realized that forgetting was not a prerequisite for forgiving, it was as if someone flipped a switch in her mind. Once Margaret began to see her pain as a testimony to what she had survived and overcame, her mindset began to change. Remembering what we've endured can be a great source of strength and gratefulness.

What About You?

That's all we know about Margaret's story, but what about your story? Will you forgive the person or people who hurt you, whether intentionally or not? What would it take for you to free them from your unforgiveness now? It's your decision. Let them go. Let God handle their judgment, whatever that may mean. Besides, you would want to be forgiven if the shoe was on the other foot, wouldn't you? So have mercy. Forgiveness is the first step to your new life. Forgiveness is golden.

2

Forgraceness Is Platinum

To forgive is golden. To *forgrace* is platinum.

Forgraceness is a clumsy term that joins together the sweet concepts of grace and forgiveness taught by Jesus Christ, the giver of life and hope. Forgraceness is the heart and guts of what I call the platinum rule. The application of the platinum rule results in forgraceness—the art of redemptive forgiveness—which transforms us from being the victim of another's negative actions to becoming a vessel of grace through whom God channels his higher purposes.

While forgiveness is letting go of our right to seek revenge, forgraceness is the extraordinary extension of goodness to bless those who have hurt us for the purpose of true redemption. It is the practical application of the platinum rule, which stands heads above the golden rule.

Notice what Jesus says in Luke 6:35-36. He goes beyond the golden rule, which many religions teach. Jesus takes the golden rule and goes platinum with it. The platinum rule extends beyond loving our neighbor or treating others as we want to be treated. The platinum rule calls us to love our enemies and pray for our persecutors. Jesus said, "Love your enemies, do good to those who hate you, bless those who curse you, pray for those who mistreat you" (Luke 6:27-28). *Wow!* Seriously, Lord? Jesus' teaching here is otherworldly. After making such a bold assertion, Jesus pokes holes in the golden rule. He says, "If you love those who love you, what credit is that to you? Even 'sinners' love those who love them" (Luke 6:32).

Forgraceness is a platinum act because it doesn't do something we would expect, like loving those who love us back. Forgraceness is going beyond expectations into the seemingly ridiculous. Yet God shows up in the realm of ridiculous. Living the golden rule is hard enough for me, but living the platinum rule takes divine enablement.

A Higher-Level Metal

When I was young I was under the impression that gold was the ultimate metal for rings, necklaces and bracelets. I was so happy when I was able to afford a 14-karat gold rope necklace. As I got older I learned that the greater the karat the more valuable the jewelry. Therefore, in my immature quest to display "bling," the next level would be an 18-karat necklace. For a while, I thought white gold would satisfy my desires. Who knew about platinum? Clearly, I didn't.

Around my college years I began to hear more about platinum. When record albums soared to the top of the charts, they didn't just go gold—they went platinum. That was indeed the pinnacle of success in sales. In my younger student years, whenever I would shop for jewelry to impress a lady, platinum rings were the most expensive (and least affordable).

The Platinum Rule in Practice

My friend Eric used to let people live with him. I was always amazed at how Eric would open his home to people. Of course many people, probably some of you, have allowed others to live with them during hard times, as Amber and I have. Maybe that is not so heroic, but Eric had a wife and several young kids at the time, and they were living in a Baltimore city apartment.

The person Eric allowed to live with him was also married with six kids. Eric, a devoted Christian man, believed that he and his wife were called to serve others no matter the cost. Eric shared with me that he felt called to allow this other family to live with him since they were in need.

I remember saying to Eric, "Man, you really are a loving brother. I've seldom seen someone love so openly and consistently as you." Eric responded in a way that both instructed and humbled me. He said, "David, this is nothing. Having someone that I love live with me is expected. If I want to be like Jesus, then the real question is, could I do this for my enemy or someone I don't like? That's the real test of my faith and love. Therefore, I still have a long way to go."

Eric was living at a level of grace and love that I had not readily considered in my own life. He was not measuring his acts from a human, golden rule level. He was measuring his acts at a platinum level—going beyond what is expected to what is only enabled by divine strength.

This Jesus kind of love makes me ask myself, *Could I bless someone who was cursing me or pray for (not against) someone who was mistreating me?* Jesus taught that even the pagans love those who love them back, or loan to those from whom they expect repayment. But the platinum level is loving our enemies and giving to others without expecting repayment. Eric captured this concept by realizing that he was living out the golden rule, but not yet the platinum rule. I'm still working on the golden rule! I want to go platinum one day.

A Biblical Example of Forgraceness

Remember Joseph in the Old Testament Scriptures (see Genesis 37–50)? Here is a young man who was hated by his older brothers and left for dead in a cistern. When a foreign group of travelers passed by, the brothers' jealous and evil hearts thought it better to sell Joseph into slavery. When Joseph went missing, the brothers concocted an alibi, saying he was killed by wild animals.

Although things got worse before they got better, because of several gracious turns in Joseph's life he eventually became the second in political command over all of Egypt. During a time of famine across the Middle East, Egypt was the only place that had food and goods to prosper. This all happened under Joseph's leadership and was sanctioned by God's amazing grace in his life. People from around the region were journeying to Egypt to get food. One such group included Joseph's brothers!

Joseph had the perfect opportunity to get back at his brothers. He could have crushed them in their weakened state of begging and weariness. As time passed Joseph's brothers no longer recognized Joseph. The last time they saw him, he was a disheveled seventeen-year-old sold into slavery. Now he is older, finely garbed and has royal authority.

Joseph extends care to his brothers and then reveals himself to them. Fearful, the brothers fully expect the righteous revenge of Joseph to be swiftly exacted on them. In fact they said to one another, "What if Joseph holds a grudge against us and pays us back for all the wrongs we did to him?" (Genesis 50:15). Joseph's brothers knew what they deserved. Retaliation was warranted.

However, Joseph says, "It was not you who sent me here, but God" (Genesis 45:8). In other words, Joseph wasn't going to hold his brothers' sins against them even though they plotted to kill him and eventually sold him into slavery. Notice Joseph's response to his brothers:

> Joseph said to them, "Don't be afraid. Am I in the place of God? You intended to harm me, but God intended it for good to accomplish what is now being done, the saving of many lives. So then, don't be afraid. I will provide for you and your children." And he reassured them and spoke kindly to them. (Genesis 50:19-21)

Unbelievable! Observe that Joseph not only forgives but he forgraces! Joseph doesn't simply spare the lives of his brothers, which is merciful and forgiving, but he forgraces by extending to them several kind acts they do not deserve.

Better Than Eric and Joseph

I can't say that I have attained the level of my friend Eric or the biblical character of Joseph when it comes to going platinum. But there is one who is the perfect example of the platinum rule, Jesus. He is our ultimate hero and the perfect model of how to live at the platinum level. I need Jesus in order to express the high calling of one who forgraces. The call is divine and unattainable by human effort. But then again, God has never called us to do something of great significance that he doesn't empower us to do.

The Platinum Prayer

Here is a prayer that might get us close to forgraceness in a practical sense.

> Dear God, without you it is hard to forgive. Without you it is impossible to forgrace. I know that I am in need of your forgiveness over and over again. Father, please empower me to forgive regularly and enable me to forgrace supernaturally. Help me to be kind like you to even the meanest people, not for my sake but for yours. May the record of my life go platinum. In Jesus' name, amen.

3

Grace Is Unfair

Grace doesn't make sense. It's too good to be true. Grace is defined as unmerited and unearned favor. It's extra goodness that is bestowed on us by God for no good reason. We don't deserve it, can't earn or repay it. It's crazy. Yet, this is what God gives to us every day. *Gracism,* a term I coined a few years ago, means to extend grace to others because of or in spite of color, class or culture. God extends grace to the human race because we are in such need of his extra favor. He is the biggest gracist of us all.

The fact that we are alive, can read and can enjoy a book like this (or endure it!) is a grace that we should thank God for. His grace is all over the place. The air we breathe, the sun we feel, the moon and the stars we appreciate, and the oceans and mountains we take in—all grace. Then when we think of the rebellion and sinful behavior we commit against God and others, it is overwhelming that God would even give us the time of day. But he does. It's amazing grace!

Beyond Forgiveness to Forgraceness

God extends grace to us beyond forgiveness. While forgiveness cleans us up and makes us right before God, grace is the extra goodness that puts a smile on our face again. God desires that we not only experience his forgiveness (because of mercy) but he wants us to smile again (because of his grace).

Likewise, when we extend grace to others beyond forgiveness, we are partaking in redemption and healing that becomes a testimony of God's grace, defying human logic. Grace beyond forgiveness is forgraceness, which is the practical application of the platinum rule.

Forgraceness is the act of extending grace that goes beyond forgiveness to people who have hurt us or caused us pain. Beyond forgiveness, forgraceness beckons us to be kind to our offender and even seek his or her well-being.

You must think it crazy to suggest such outrageous behavior. You are right; I can't believe that I am extolling this otherworldly concept. It is nearly impossible to imagine. There is something incredibly redemptive and divine about such mysterious behavior. I am writing about a concept that is above my pay grade and, frankly, my own ability to consistently apply.

How is it that people who have been violated and betrayed could actually wish the best for their perpetrator? How could an unforgivable act result in a gracious result? Someone once said that we have seen a real miracle when we have witnessed a man or woman who is fully surrendered to God. Forgraceness takes full surrender and divine enablement.

God wants to know if we are willing to forgrace others. He will strengthen us. King David said,

> It is God who arms me with strength
>   and makes my way perfect. (2 Samuel 22:33)

None of us can forgrace in our own strength, but God teaches us that in our weakness he is strong (2 Corinthians 12:10).

If people are left in awe because your forgraceness has been expressed, then you can be sure that God has shown up in a mysterious way through your weakness. Putting a smile on the face of someone we would rather see cry and perhaps wince in pain is not human in nature, but godly. God's desire is that his redemptive power leads others to smile in awe of his grace. God is the ultimate forgracer.

Forgraceness on a Personal Note

On a smaller scale I have witnessed God's divine
work in my own life. As a pastor you can imagine
that I take a lot of criticism. There are some people
who simply lack tact and sensitivity.

A few years ago a woman left our church after
using many of the ministries within the church to
meet her social and spiritual needs. This woman
made me and others aware that she would not be
giving money to our capital campaign project because she was unhappy with the church (again!).
Her mouth often got her in trouble, and over the
years she had managed to ostracize many servants
in the church. Yet she wondered why she didn't fit
in. Upon her departure she announced that she
was leaving the church because she no longer believed in my leadership. Whenever people leave
Bridgeway, I do my best to bless them with a sense
of grace on their way out the door. While peeved
by this woman's actions, I blessed her with well
wishes and kept the door open for her to return
one day by saying, "Should the Lord bring you
back to Bridgeway, I want you to know that the
door is always open."

As time passed I had forgotten about this
woman. But after I finished preaching one Sun-
day, I was moving toward the side steps to exit the
stage and guess who was waiting in the line to

greet me? Yes, it was her.

"Jesus, help me now" was my quick prayer! This woman wanted a friendly greeting, and, frankly, I wanted to act like I didn't see her. Of course I knew exactly what God was prompting me to do. But inside I was protesting, *Shoot, this is just not fair.* I ranted in my heart and mind, *Lord, why do people get to come and go to church as they please, use up the ministries that build into them, and then say whatever they want on their way out? Why can't I say a word or two about their backbiting, ungrateful, self-centered, gossiping selves?* That is not a very forgracing heart, is it? God is still working on me!

God made me aware that grace is not fair. In fact, grace is unfair and gives beyond what is just or right. It lavishes goodness beyond the measure of exact accounting. To take it a step further, the same words I was thinking about this woman were probably true of me as they related to how I treat God. Yet, he has been more than gracious to me, time and again. So who am I to withhold grace from others?

With this internal discourse going on in my heart and mind about how I wanted nothing to do with this lady, I reached out my arms and hugged her when I got to the bottom of the steps. I told her how nice it was to see her again. (Okay, maybe I wasn't completely honest.)

The lady shared, "Pastor, I have been struggling with my health, and emotionally I have been struggling with depression. Would you please pray for me?" I realized that God was calling me to be a forgracer in that moment, not a scorekeeper, nor simply a forgiver. God was encouraging me to go beyond forgiveness into forgraceness, extending favor and goodness beyond forgiveness. While living out the platinum rule of redemption by ministering to this daughter of God, I discovered that I too was being healed and freed from my own hurt. Only God!

Fairness Is Overrated

I suppose if God were basing his grace toward me on the scale of fairness, I would have been exterminated a long time ago. I could never stand up to God's scale of fairness. I thank God that none of us are judged according to fairness. Who could stand?

In Psalm 103 we are told that God does not treat us as our sins deserve. He is long-suffering, very kind and gracious beyond what any of us deserve. The Bible teaches that God is "compassionate and gracious, slow to anger, abounding in love" (Psalm 103:8). The next time we want to hold others to the standard of fairness, let's remember that fairness is overrated and grace is unfair. Sometimes I just bow my head in prayer and say, "Thank you, God, for not being fair in your judgment of me."

4

I Love You Dearly

Words matter, but actions make them matter more. I frequently tell my wife that I love her. I say it to my kids often. We often speak words of love as a family. Amber has said to me on more than one occasion, "David, you have got to demonstrate your love, not just say it." The value behind words comes when we back them up with action.

In chapter three we talked about Joseph, who forgave and refused to take revenge on his brothers. Yet we see that Joseph did more than forgive; he forgraced. Joseph demonstrated kindness to his backstabbing family members in very practical ways. You see, I believe that Joseph loved his brothers dearly. Even though they hurt him deeply, Joseph's heart was overflowing with love for his brothers.

Have you ever loved someone even though this person has done nothing but hurt you deeply over and over again? What a conflict of the heart. I believe this is exactly how Joseph felt when he saw his hurtful brothers face to face. Joseph had every right to beat his brothers down and make them pay for their mean-spirited acts of harm, yet Joseph loved his brothers and couldn't hold a grudge. (Why is it that the ones we love the most can at times hurt us the deepest?)

Notice what Genesis 45:14-15 says after Joseph reveals his identity to his unsuspecting brothers. "Then he threw his arms around his brother Benjamin and wept, and Benjamin embraced him, weeping. And he kissed all his brothers and wept over them. Afterward his brothers talked with him." Wow. Does this sound like a man who had been disrespected and discarded? No.

Joseph probably had many days, months and years of great heartache, anger and regret. Who knows, maybe deep in his heart he even desired to get even with his brothers, but revenge was nowhere to be found. Joseph's love emerged.

Often, I believe, under layers of hurt and pain we too still have love for those who have hurt us. Once we forgive them we may actually remember why it was that we loved them so much in the first place. We learn in the story of Joseph that love is more than a feeling, and is properly expressed in very practical ways. Joseph demonstrated love for his brothers through three acts of forgraceness.

Three Practical Acts of Forgraceness

1. Calm fears. First, Joseph calms their fears of judgment and retaliation. He says, "Don't be afraid" (Genesis 50:19). When we have forgiven someone, the first act of forgraceness is to give them a calming word to let them know that we will not retaliate, even when it seems justified. Joseph could do this because he knew that God was in total control of his life, and that vengeance belongs solely to God. He recognized that the evil done to him with bad intentions was ordained and overseen by God for a larger purpose that would ultimately propel Joseph into a place of blessing.

What about you? Can you extend forgiveness to your enemies because you trust God to be your righteous judge who can make sense of every bad experience with his sovereign hand? Would you be willing to calm your enemies so they are not afraid of you? Extending an olive branch of safety to a fearful enemy is a practical act of forgraceness.

Let your adversaries know that they need not fear you. When they see your faith in God, they will at some point have to realize that they must contend with him, not you, because the favor of God is on you.

2. *Extend favor.* The second act of Joseph's forgraceness is that he extends favor to his brothers' children. Joseph says, "I will provide for you and your children" (Genesis 50:21). Joseph's kindness extended beyond forgiving his brothers to offering generosity to their families as well.

What kind of world would we live in if enemies had mercy on their opponents and then provided care for their opponents' offspring? This may seem impossible, but when God gives us the power over our opponents and we choose not to crush them but to bless them, we have learned the art of redemptive forgiveness. We have gone platinum. This is a forgiveness that goes beyond the mercy of nonretaliation. It extends to acts of kindness to the person or people who hurt us.

What about you? Have you ever thought about extending extra grace and favor to the ones who have hurt you? Is there something you can do that will communicate to them that they no longer have to fear your anger or revenge? If they need a cup of cold water, would you be able to compassionately give them a bucket instead of throwing it on them? This is so hard. This is so platinum.

3. *Kind words.* The third act of forgraceness that Joseph expressed was kind words. Joseph had

every right to verbally lambaste his brothers. I'm
sure if you are like me, you have struggled with
wanting to give someone who has hurt or betrayed
you a "piece of your mind." You have rehearsed in
your head several times what you would say if you
had the chance. Well, Joseph had the opportunity
to seize his moment of sweet revenge as he faced
his brothers. He could have given a speech to the
nation about how his brothers threw him in a cistern and sold him into slavery. He could have em-
barrassed them and announced that their current
weakness and poverty was God's judgment on
them for their heinous acts.

Many of us might be tempted to speak words of
judgment at this point and feel justified in doing
so. This would be the perfect time to let his brothers have it. Joseph had God's favor, and his brothers were now in the position of worms. Poetic justice, right? Maybe so, but Joseph was having none
of it. He lived through the difficulties of trial and
tragedy, and was not willing to be imprisoned by
unforgiveness or drink the bitter gall of resentment. Instead, he chose to speak life instead of
death: "And he reassured them and spoke kindly
to them" (Genesis 50:21).

Joseph spoke kindly to his brothers. He not only
gave calming words and provided for his brothers
and their families, but he reassured them that he

could be trusted to do the same in the future. He
would not stab them in the back later. He vowed to
them that his kindness wasn't a ploy to set them up
for a later beating. Joseph was a forgracer. Joseph
went platinum.

What About You?

When was the last time you've spoken with your
adversaries or opponents? When the opportunity
arises, will you speak kindly to them? I know it's
hard, but this is the secret to living free and being
empowered to soar above your hurt and pain. You
can wallow in the cistern of your past and recount
the pain of your slavery, or you can choose to rise
above your wounds and be a gracist, a forgracer.
No person, even someone who has hurt you, can
take away your joy, your song or your peace unless
you surrender it. They cannot rob you of the grace
to be kind, forgiving and positive. Come on, let go
of the past by choosing to speak kindly from this
point on. You can cancel the bad with good, and
you can cancel death with life.

Turnaround

You will discover that the evil intentions of others
cannot overcome God's ultimate purpose and
plans for you. They will only be used in the manu-

script of your overall storyline. Hence, what was meant for evil will be turned and leveraged for redemptive good (Genesis 50:20). God is perfect when it comes to turnarounds. He can take what was meant to break you, and use it to remake you. He can make you better, stronger and even more gracious than before.

Will you allow God to turn your anger to forgiveness? Will you ask God to turn your frustration to laughter and your mourning to dancing? He can do it because your God is in the turnaround business. He simply needs a willing heart. Agree?

Say "I forgrace you!" Like Joseph, is it possible that you still love the person or people who injured you? Maybe the love never stopped. Maybe it just got buried under all the hurt and pain of their transgressions against you. As your heart begins to melt with forgiveness and forgraceness, you may honestly be able to say "I love you dearly." Still.

Back It Up

Joseph backed up his kind words with loving actions of support by making provisions for his brothers and their families in a practical way, with food and protection. And Amber continually encourages me to demonstrate my love beyond words. Don't get me wrong; she likes the words. In fact, I'm really good at words. I not only tell her that I love her dearly, but I write it and sing it too. However, the power of the words has so much more substance when they are accompanied by consistent behavior that underscores my rhetoric. Otherwise, it's simply verbiage.

In our household one of the things I truly hate is doing the financial books. Amber has been doing them for years, and I was the "overseer," if you will. But I didn't take into account the great weight of responsibility and anxiety this placed on Amber. After fifteen years I finally did something that is against the grain of every fiber in my being. I took over the books.

This may sound weird to some, but the act of doing our financial books has not only relieved my wife's bookkeeping anxiety but in an unexpected way it has communicated practical love and care. It is, she says, "proactive and protective."

I suppose we could look at such an example as small. But saying "I love you dearly" is not always about the grand actions. Often it is demonstrated through small, consistent acts of commitment, especially when rebuilding trust. Keep saying "I love you," but make sure you back it up!

5

I Apologize Sincerely

Who should say "I'm sorry"? Often in conflict we have so entangled our emotions and compounded offenses it becomes difficult to know who is at fault. Blaming others becomes easy, and justifying our own inappropriateness becomes normal, if not epidemic.

Because Amber and I have dealt with difficulties that have caused us to look at the other as a terrible, sinning monster, I understand the temptation to point the finger. I'm sure she has had reasons to point at me at least once, maybe twice. Okay, I stopped counting after our first week of marriage. In the finger-pointing duels that take place, who should apologize first when we are both exclaiming, "It is your fault"?

I have a good number of friends, family and

church members who are divorced. When the subject of their divorce comes up, I hear many stories of how bad the "ex" is. I have made it a habit to ask divorced persons I'm speaking with, "What percentage of the marital breakdown do you accept fault for?" This question is very helpful because over time the ex-spouse is blamed for everything. Seldom have I heard someone who is divorced say, "I screwed up and lost my spouse because of what I contributed to the breakdown of the relationship."

I pose this question because it usually takes two to come together and two to mess things up. When they own their percentage of the problem, people can move on, even when the other person was 95 percent at fault and turned out to be a complete donkey's hind end. Owning 5 percent of the fault may be the difference in not making the same mistake again.

Having said this, I am aware that some people *are* victimized for no fault of their own and should be excluded from this example. I am simply attempting to help people who have a problem seeing their own sin to learn the wonderful and freeing habit of confession. As the old saying goes, when you point the finger at someone, you still have three fingers pointing back at you.

Jesus put it another way, "Why do you look at the speck of sawdust in your brother's eye and pay no attention to the plank in your own eye?" (Matthew 7:3). Jesus is encouraging us to pay attention to our percentage of the problem, and to own up to what we have contributed to the negative situation, lest we become hypocritical in seeing everyone else's faults but our own.

Confession is God's gift to us to mend relationships. When we have failed God, we should admit it and ask for mercy. In addition, when we have hurt, injured or offended others, let's just admit it. Say, "I am so sorry. I was wrong. Please forgive me."

When we do this, we minister to the people we have offended by reminding them that they are not crazy for being angry with us. When we apologize for our 5 or 50 or 100 percent of wrongdoing, we make ourselves vulnerable to the other person, which can be a bit scary at times, but it is God's pathway to reconciliation.

How Should I Apologize?

Find an appropriate time and a safe place to communicate to the person (or persons) you have offended. Tell him or her what you have done (to the degree that is appropriate) and then say, "I am so sorry. I messed up. I was wrong. Will you please forgive me?"

You can say this in writing, on the phone or face to face, but say it—you must. The words are healing for the offended and the offender. When you apologize, you are doing it because it is right. It is fair and freeing. When apologizing it is important to think through what you contributed to the hurt, and verbalize that to the person you are apologizing to. By doing this you are communicating to the other person that you understand the weight and exact nature of the offense. In addition, while apologies in one-on-one relationships should be as specific as possible, group apologies should be thought out carefully because of gossip and misunderstanding. It may be wise to be general with information but sincere with a spirit of humility.

Telephone apologies are not best, but are sometimes necessary. Generally speaking, I think it is much better to apologize on the phone and promise to follow up face to face than to let too much time go by until you see the person. If you are texting an apology, use the same rule as the telephone. I propose that you text the apology and promise to follow up in person. Do not think that the phone or a text is final. That is a myth. People need to see our eyes and sense our spirit to seal the connection. If you write a letter on paper or send an e-mail, the details of your apology can be written out, and the recipient can sit with your words before responding. This can be a good approach to apologizing for deeper hurts. Ongoing correspondence over time and letters can give space for emotions and prayers to settle. There may need to be several sets of letters before a face-to-face meeting is welcome. One caution: what you write in a letter or e-mail can be read by other parties or forwarded. So be wise and aware.

Whatever the reason for apologizing and asking for forgiveness, remember this rule: your apology is to serve the other person, not just assuage your guilt. Hence, to benefit the recipient, consider the timing and his or her emotional readiness.

Giving Up Power

Once you have apologized, it's up to the other person whether or not to forgive you. Sometimes the person will forgive and sometimes he or she won't, but at least you did your part by sincerely seeking forgiveness. Because you are placing the power to forgive in the other party's hand once you apologize, it may become uncomfortable to wait for a response. This is the exact reason why so many fail to apologize. Their pride will not allow the other person to see them vulnerable or allow the other person to have the power of choice. They seek to control the relationship and hence refuse to apologize. As a result, they have indeed remained in control, but they do so at the expense of abiding discord and unreconciled relationships.

Another reason some fail to apologize is because they realize that changed behavior (or some other consequence) naturally accompanies a sincere apology. If I apologize for stealing, it will most likely mean that I will have to return or repay what I stole. A person who is sincerely sorry will stand ready to accept the consequences of his or her actions while appealing for whatever mercy is needed.

Getting Practical

If you want to sincerely apologize to someone, give the person this book and highlight the following statement. Below the statement write from your heart in your own words whatever you need to express to communicate your remorse and repentance.

Statement of Apology

Dear _____:

I am so sorry for what I did or said. There is no excuse for my action(s) and I sincerely apologize to you. Will you please forgive me? If you do, I will be grateful to you for letting me off the hook and not holding my wrongdoing and sin against me. I will do my best to not repeat my actions so I will not knowingly injure you again. In addition, I am willing to do what I must to make our situation right. Let me know what that is, and I will do my best to accept the consequences of my sin in order to reconcile with you.

I am also requesting something from you. Will you "forgrace" me? This may take prayer on your part because the request is something I do not deserve. By forgracing me, you are committing to extending goodness and favor toward me to demonstrate the loving redemption that comes from the power of Jesus Christ. I don't deserve your goodness toward me, and I cannot repay it after what I have done to hurt you, but if you will forgrace me, I will do my best to pay it forward to others and to return gratitude in whatever feeble ways I can. Finally, whether you forgive and forgrace me or not, I still want you to know that I am sincerely sorry for my offense. In addition to what I've highlighted, I have handwritten a personal note to you:

_____

_____

_____

_____

_____

_____

_____

_____

_____

_____

_____

_____

Very sincerely,

_____

A Platinum Vision for
Race Relations in America

Speaking of apologies, I've been pondering a platinum idea as it relates to race in America. May I
share it with you?

Take a deep breath and ponder the next sentence slowly. What would happen if African Amer-
icans in our country organized and came together
to tell white America "We forgive and forgrace
you"?

What would happen if blacks officially forgave
whites for all the past hurts, pains, enslavement
and discrimination? What would happen if we
said, "Father, forgive them for they know not what
they do"?

I believe that the sweetness of forgiveness and
forgraceness that is associated with the name of
Jesus would be accompanied by the powerful
movement of the Holy Spirit on earth, and we
would see reconciliation at a spiritual level that has

not been known. It would free blacks and whites. It would usher in a new era of revival that we have not yet seen. It would bring healing.

Then, what would happen if whites received the forgiveness and forgraceness, and responded with "Thank you"? If whites showed their gratitude for the forgraceness that has been extended to them, it would heal and seal the relationship.

When we have healing and sealing, we can move on to a new level of destiny that has for too long escaped us. Forgraceness is God's path to redemption. I wish with all of my heart that the power of such redemption would unite blacks, whites and others in the United States.

6

You've Hurt Me Deeply

After eating a meal together our family throws away our scraps in Tupperware bins on the kitchen counter. My wife has instructed the kids and me not to throw away banana peels, apple rinds, coffee grounds, egg shells and the like into the garbage. She wants it all on the counter in the Tupperware. Can you imagine the smell of old and rotting food scraps sitting out for a day or two or three on the kitchen counter? Yuck! Shortly after Amber realized that the Tupperware wasn't good enough to contain the scraps, she bought a marble container with a perfect top for such matter.

Do you know why my wife collects these scraps?

Composting. That's right, my wife likes to compost. I didn't even know what a composter was until Amber started dumping these scraps into black containers we have the in backyard. The yucky scraps in the composter spoil day after day as Amber periodically tills its contents. Over time the tilled spoil turns into a rich, dark fertilizer that she adds to the soil in her garden and flower beds.

She tells me that this "fertilizer" is the best agent for her garden. It is naturally rich in nutrients and gives better life to the soil as her vegetables and fruit grow. She says that this fertilizer, made from scraps, is also known as "black gold."

As a black man, after hearing this rich description, I couldn't help but say to Amber, who happens to be a racially mixed Korean woman, "See, baby, you married black gold." She responded quickly, "Yeah, men are dirt." We both laughed. Of course, all men are not dirt, but I got the point.

The Dirt on Me

Speaking of dirt, maybe this would be an appropriate time to be honest with you about my struggles. Shamefully, I admit to you that I have done some impure things that have not been honoring to God or my wife. From the time I was a teenager through my young adult years and even throughout the first chapters of our marriage I've struggled with being pure before God in mind and body. Amber and I have struggled with how to love and honor one another for two decades. After much hurt, many tough conversations, betrayals between us in ways that we share only with each other and our counselors, we have gone through many "dangers, toils and snares," so to speak.

The good news is that I can humbly report to you that today Amber and I have never been closer to one another emotionally and spiritually than we are now. We more than love each other. We actually *like* each other. It used to be this way in the early years of our romance, but after marriage, ministry and our blessed rugrats (kids), we drifted apart for so many reasons that we both accept blame for.

A Nonplatinum Marriage Rating

Years ago when we sought help, the counselor asked us to rate our marriage on a scale of 1 to 10. A 10 meant fantastically connected in every way. A 1 meant dead, lifeless—a marriage that completely stinks. How does a man answer such a question in front of his wife? Whatever you say, you simply cannot win. Therefore, I decided that honesty was the best policy and blurted out, "I rate our marriage at a 2."

I swallowed deeply, glanced over to Amber, who would barely look in my direction. Then the counselor turned to Amber for her answer. She said, "I would give our marriage a negative 2." Yikes! That wasn't even on the scale! Dang, that hurt. But it was true.

Can you imagine a marriage surviving such a low rating while in the crucible of church ministry with its attendant public scorn? Can you imagine everyone giving their opinion about what you should do with your spouse, your ministry, your kids and your life? Can you imagine the embarrassment of people talking, probing, gossiping, and even plotting and campaigning against you and the ministry? At times, such a life felt completely worthless.

Remember the Scraps?

But wait; remember the scraps on the kitchen counter? That's all we had—scraps. We had the scraps of a marriage and ministry. Together Amber and I decided to put the scraps of our lives in the composter of God's care. With elders who cared about our well-being and friends who were committed to us more than our public ministry; and with counselors who were paid to listen, advise and treat our "business" in confidence, we agreed to jump into the composter together with all of our scraps and trust God with the outcome.

At least we were together. We held on to each other and to God. Amber and I covenanted to cling to each other regardless of what anyone else said. We were willing to give up our ministry, our reputations and our aspirations. The only thing we cared about was our family and whatever dignity we had left. Other than that, we didn't give a Hoover Dam about what others said about us or how bad our scraps smelled. We knew that if we were in the care of God's composting will, he would take care of us.

Over the next couple of years transformation and redemption were coming about. It was slow and took plenty of time, hundreds of conversations, raw and revolving emotions, and lots of care from others, but Amber and I were changing. A metamorphosis was happening as we held onto each other and God held onto us. The deep hurts we caused each other were being healed. We were listening to each other and understanding why we did and said the things we did. We began to "get" each other and empathetically comprehend each other's truth. Throughout the journey God was transforming our scraps into black gold.

Cucumber

Something surprising happened as Amber was growing squash, tomatoes, cantaloupe and strawberries in her garden. A cucumber started to grow, and then another, and another. This was quite sur-

prising to us because Amber never planted cucum-
bers, at least not on purpose. Evidently, in the
midst of the black gold were seeds of an unexpected vegetable.

We had a fat cucumber we didn't plant but could
now cut up and eat at our kitchen table. And we
did! Amber said to the family when we sat down
for dinner, "Look at this big, healthy cucumber
from my garden." We were all amazed at how
plump and juicy that cucumber was, and it tasted
so fresh!

The point is clear, isn't it? When we submit our
life experiences into his hands, God can produce
unexpected fruit out of our lives. Scraps and messes
that others would dispose of as garbage (even us),
God can use to demonstrate his miracles of grace.

Did you know that God can make a big, fat and
juicy cucumber out of your mess?

As a result, no one gets the glory but God. No
one can explain the miracle of your dirt. God, in
his divine way, takes our ashes and trades them for
beauty. He can take the black gold of our lives to
nourish others with a sense of authenticity and organic sincerity that can't be fabricated or produced
with pretense. It is real and it is fresh.

That is exactly how Amber and I would describe
our marriage. Real and fresh. Not perfect but real,
tasty, fruitful, organic and miraculous. We thank

God for the crucible of composting. It forced us to learn how to live with forgiveness and taught us how to become forgracers. We have moved beyond forgiveness, which means to let one another go, into forgraceness, which is to extend kindness and favor to each other.

As a result God, and only God, has worked the mystery of transforming our scraps into black gold, and then into fruit, vegetables and a bed of garden flowers that others can behold.

Recently, Amber and I checked our marriage ratings. We both agreed that we now rate our marriage at an 8.5. Wow! Is that amazing or what? Only God could take us from a failing grade to a B. How did we get there? *Forgraceness*—from God and from each other. We are still striving for an A. Forgraceness will get us there one day, I pray.

Your Hurt

My appeal to you is to give your scraps to God—your hurt, pain, disappointments and so on. Only God can bring life to that which is dead. Has someone hurt you deeply? Have you hurt someone? Have you been wounded to the core of your being? God understands even when those who hurt you don't.

You can forgive them. God has given you the power. Let them go from the prison of your unfor-

giving heart and plunge yourself into the composter of God's will. If you allow him to work with you
and if you cooperate with his will, over time you
will discover that you are transforming into a completely different you. It will not always be painless,
but it will always produce a greater result than the
current scraps you may now be living with. Do not
throw away your pain. God will never waste it if
you give it to him.

God's Secret to Redemption

Did you know that God has given you the power to
be kind and even generous to the those who hurt
you deeply? You can be gracious to them. It is
counterintuitive because everything in you may
want to hurt them back, but God calls us to bless
those who curse us, and to not return insult with
insult but with blessing. Why? Because that is the
secret of forgraceness. Through blessing others
with grace beyond what they deserve, God shows
up in us and heals our hearts with a redemptive
portion of recovery.

   If God can save my marriage and create something more beautiful than before, then he can re-
deem what you have lost. There is hope, and that
hope is in God. He will bring new fruit out of your
hurt. But first, you must give it to him and then
cooperate with his composting will in your life.

7

I'm Concerned About You Personally

Do you know someone who is dying inside because of anger, bitterness, contempt and resentment? Are you concerned about him or her? It is true that we need counselors, doctors and medication to help us with medical, psychological and chemical ailments. Likewise, our souls need emotional and spiritual medicine to heal our hearts. Forgraceness is a spiritual medicine that will bring healing to painfully ailing hearts.

Going beyond forgiving others by extending gracious acts of kindness and compassion to them is a healing balm that many fail to experience. There is a redemptive spiritual and medicinal effect when we, like Jesus, offer grace to the most undeserving. However, the greatest problem that we face is our own anger, bitterness and uncanny ability to turn holding a grudge into an art form. Consequently, when holding grudges toward others, we are actually inflicting damage on ourselves.

How Do We Get Justice When We Want to Strangle Someone?

Amber and I have been trying to become debt free. In an attempt to reach this goal we decided to stop leasing Amber's car, which had been a monthly expense in our budget for many years. Summer had come and it was time for us to turn in her minivan for another vehicle. In the past, after three years we would normally turn in the keys to our leased vehicle only to be handed a new set of keys for a brand-new car.

This time, however, we turned in our keys and walked away. Off to the used-car dealers we went. We shopped and kicked tires until we found the perfect used car for Amber—so we thought. It was a preowned midsized SUV that was several years old but seemed to be running well. The dealer assured us that the vehicle was in good working condition, the state inspection sticker certified that the car had passed, and Amber really enjoyed the idea of an SUV instead of the leased minivans she had been driving for a decade.

Excited about not having a car payment, we

filled out the paperwork and gave the used-car dealer a down payment. Within a few days we were able to drive the car off of the lot. Within four months we completely paid off the vehicle. I was so happy about reaching this goal—until things on the car started breaking down. The lock on the back door worked only intermittently. Then the steering wheel began to shake. We immediately called the dealer and returned the car to be fixed.

A week later, water started seeping inside the car on the passenger-side floor. After returning it for correction, it happened again. This was so frustrating. Within a five month period, we had to return the car six times. The inconvenience of having a new used car that was continually in need of attention was disheartening to say the least. The last straw was when the car would randomly decide not to start and could not accelerate beyond thirty miles per hour without shaking violently. Of course this would usually happen at the most inconvenient times, like when it is time to go to work, church or in the middle of an impending East Coast snow storm!

We chose to take the car to a different dealer and paid to have it fully examined. That dealer quoted us several thousand dollars of work that would need to be done should we want the vehicle to drive correctly. We were dismayed.

I called the owner of the car dealership who sold us the car and told him of our experience and how unhappy we were. He assured me that if I brought the car in (again!), his shop would fix it. What we thought would take days to repair took weeks, and much inconvenience. But, here's the kicker, the dealer said that they could fix everything on the car but we would have to pay for it. That's right, a car that I paid for in full and that had been returned repeatedly is now going to cost me even more money. I was livid.

We simply wanted a vehicle that would drive correctly for the money we paid. Was that too much to ask? Evidently for this dealer it was. The customer service was bad; we were mad. But we swallowed hard and paid the money. Argh!

After three weeks of waiting for a well-working vehicle (one could only hope), the dealer called to tell us that the car was ready for pick up. Unfortunately, I had to catch a flight and was unable to join my wife in retrieving the car. By the time I had reached my destination and began to deplane, I had received a call from Amber. She was in possession of the car but reported to me, in a very upset tone, that the contents she had left in the car were all stolen, including all of her CDs as well as my twelve-year-old son's iPod, which he left in the glove compartment.

She called the dealer, and they basically told Amber, "Oh well, there's nothing we could do. We are not responsible for things you left in your car." What a comedy of errors this was becoming. Does it really cost this much to become debt free, I wondered!

Anyway, I personally called the owner from the city I was in to talk about our disappointment with the vehicle, the service and of course the stolen property. His response was much like the others at the dealership, "Sorry, we can't be responsible for the safety of your car."

I have to admit that I wanted to reach through the phone and strangle this guy. How's that for being a forgracing Christian man? I was becoming angrier just speaking with the dealer on the phone; not to mention that my wife was home seething as my son cried over his stolen iPod.

Have you ever felt rage building inside of you toward someone else because what they said or did upset you? I don't mean to imply violence, and I am not meaning to advocate strangling in the literal sense. What I'm really saying is that there are points in our lives when we get angry because of how others mistreat us.

There was nothing more we could do unless we wanted to picket in front of the car dealership to demonstrate to all the passersby that we bought a lemon. I'm still considering this option. (Not really.)

How can we forgive when we are so angry and feel like we have been taken advantage of? When we feel like we have been wronged and we want justice, or at least fairness, to prevail, how do we navigate our call to forgive while getting the satisfaction we deserve for the injustice experienced?

In answering this question for myself, I realized that the first thing I needed to do was stop calling this used-car dealer nasty names in my mind and to start praying for a calm spirit. But I was still left with how to handle the mishandling of my time and finances.

Maybe you find yourself in a similar situation. You have been wronged, hurt or have lost something of value because of someone else's misbehavior. Maybe your issue is much weightier than getting stuck with a lemon. It could be even worse, like a deep hurt to the heart, body and spirit. Whatever the offense, how do you get justice? You don't. God does.

Heavy-Duty Forgraceness

My car situation might qualify as a very low level of frustration in comparison to what has gone wrong in your life because of the death of a child at the hands of a drunk driver or the loss of a loved one because of a home invasion.

What about the Rwandan genocides in the last decade or the post-election violence in Kenya? This is heavy-duty stuff. Is forgraceness powerful enough to wade through the mud of such massacres?

An acquaintance of mine just returned from Rwanda and reported that he was taken around the country to see where uncounted numbers of Rwandans were left for dead because of ethnic and political war. But the amazing story is his accounts of reconciliation in which people who are grieving the loss of their loved ones have forgiven the perpetrators. Because of this real forgiveness, the perpetrators and those who have forgiven them are working together to build new villages.

Gracism in Kenya

Our partnering churches and ministries in Kenya have taken hold of the concepts of gracism. Together, our leaders and theirs have studied the principles of reconciliation and gracism so that many tribes can live in peace and unity by doing multitribal ministry. Amazingly enough, during the last outbreak of violence throughout the country, this particular town of Webuye, Kenya, did not experience one drop of blood from violence.

As a result of our brothers and sisters in Christ

building bridges of reconciliation for years, this
town became known as the village of peace. Regardless of their tribal affiliation, many in the area
fled to Webuye for safety when ethnic violence was
tearing apart the country.

While visiting Webuye a couple of months ago,
I sat with several pastors as they recounted the sad
and horrific stories of violence throughout the land.
One pastor was present at our meeting because he
had been rescued from a neighboring village. Most
of the violence happened at night, so during the
day pastors from Webuye traveled to rescue this
pastor from the tribal turmoil within his own village and within his own congregation.

Because of tribalism believers in Christ within
his own church turned on him and burned down
their own church. As he sat in on our roundtable
discussion, his only question was how to forgive
others now that he was separated from his village,
the church he had built and, most heartbreakingly,
his family members, including his wife.

I was very concerned about this pastor on an
emotional level. Spiritually, his smile was grand
and his heart was big. He simply wanted to know
how he could access this forgiveness and forgraceness that I was talking about so that he could apply
it to his situation. In light of this, who really cares
about problems with a used car?

Forgraceness is for both the smaller-level frustrations and the heaviest of loads that burden our souls. Whatever concerns you, forgraceness is God's medicine to heal you, free you and energize you back to life.

I'm Concerned About You

This chapter is for those who feel as if they are dying under the weight of great pain, anger and resentment. You should know that others are very concerned about you. They don't want you to suffer under such weight. Jesus can bear this load with you. He can help you move toward a healthier existence, but you must let go of the desire for revenge and begin to open yourself up to be a forgracer.

The following prayer was written with you in mind. Consider praying a similar prayer to help you begin the process of marrying forgiveness and grace in order to birth a new, healthier and forgracing you.

Dear God, I don't even know where to begin. I am so hurt and angry. I can't believe you allowed this to happen to me. I'm mad and confused. Please help me, Lord. Help me to process my anger toward you and others. Help me to begin to forgive those who hurt and damaged me. Please allow me to leave justice in your hands, and give me the strength to take my hands and my will off of this situation. I release my offender (or offenders) to you and will begin trusting you with him or her. I also give myself to you and trust you with my pain. By your grace, I am choosing in this prayer to forgive my offender. Help me to live out this forgiveness. Should I be given the opportunity one day, empower me to extend grace to my offender, which would take a miracle. For now, I will leave that up to you. I simply need your comfort and grace to sit with this important decision to prayerfully forgive. Thank you, Lord, for beginning this healing process in me. In Jesus' name, amen.

A New Start

Once we pray sincerely to God and do our best to lay everything at his feet, his peace begins to settle on us. When we get up from prayer we can walk away with confidence that God has our problems in his hands. Whether our challenges are huge, like wars and violent injustices, or relatively small, like relationships that break our expectations and hearts, prayer gives us an opportunity for a new start.

Challenges can be national or international, corporate or communal. In the end they all affect us personally when the trouble crosses our path. This is why personal concern for those who are hurting is the focus of this chapter.

If you are concerned about someone because you sense he or she is being eaten up inside by hurt, anger or bitterness, pass this book to the person. Have the person read the prayer above. Maybe you can read the prayer with him or her.

God desires to bring healing to our lives, and it is possible that giving someone this book will help in the process. I pray that this book is used by God to give people a new start.

8

You've Helped Me Tremendously (Thanks for Your Forgraceness in My Life)

Who do you know who has extended forgraceness to you? Are you thankful for the second, fifth or tenth chance they have given you? Hasn't their forgiveness and grace helped you tremendously to move forward and let go of the past? If so, have you said thank you?

Maybe you verbalize your gratitude. That's great! But others might say thanks through a hand-written note, by sending an e-mail or text, mailing a gift, leaving a voicemail or some other creative way. Sometimes a public thank you may be in order.

Public Thanks, Not Just Public Spanks

I was invited to a consultation at a Christian college I respect. The topic of discussion was evangelism and ethnicity. The organizers wanted me to know that my presence and voice was important and valuable to the theological and practical discussion. To my delight, after adjusting schedules, I was able to make the engagement work.

At the consultation I was both enlightened and enriched by the discussion between theorists and practitioners in the world of evangelicalism. The only down side about the consultation was that besides a professor from the college, who was a presenter, I was the only African American male in the room. There was a Native American pastor from Canada and a few international attendees from Australia and England, but that was it.

How were we going to have a rich dialogue on evangelism and ethnicity in America at an academic and practical level if there were no other American minorities besides me in the room? How fruitful, insightful and representative could the conversation be? How deep could we really get about the gospel's power in practice as it relates to Jesus' and Paul's mandates to take the gospel to unbelievers beyond the Jews?

I waited until the second day of the three-day consultation before raising my questions and concerns about this. I was hesitant to speak about my thoughts because I did not want to be the sourpuss who was raining on the parade, nor did I want to pull the race card to trump the event. The last thing I wanted was for the conveners to feel guilty when they had worked so diligently to get me to the table. I could only imagine how hard they had to work to get other African American voices to attend, but to no avail.

The moment of truth came when the topic of multiethnic evangelism was clearly teed up and at hand. Choosing my words carefully and prayerfully, I had to speak. Trying not to sound like an "angry black man" frustrated with yet another conversation about race, I shared my questions and concerns as graciously and truthfully as I could.

The next thirty to forty minutes offered a robust, inspiring conversation, which began with a response from one of the white organizers whose first words were repentance. He was very genuine in his own disappointment that more blacks and other minorities were not present at the table. He shared how hard he had worked to get them there. He shared the roadblocks and realities of his conundrum.

Out of the passionate and somewhat painful discussion came a very clear example—a case study, if you will—of why it is so difficult to get

people from different races in the same room to
have a discussion about topics that shape evangelicalism. Through this we learned that strategies,
relationships and core principles regarding multi-
culturalism matter just as much as the right heart
and hard work, both of which the organizers had.

There was no racism, insensitivity or careless-
ness involved in leaving out minorities in this particular case. It was quite the opposite. However,
the strategies and principles of the steering com-
mittee were not congruent with their heart and
hard work, hence an undesirable result.

Later in the consultation I had the opportunity to
share some of my thoughts. One of the first things I
did was to thank the conveners and others who
were there. My thanksgiving was for the opportunity I had to be enriched by the conversation, but it
was also gratitude for the openness and heartfelt
work of the organizers. Although the consultation
did not produce the multiethnic results, the efforts
were there and they needed to be affirmed.

I verbalized my gratitude. We often verbalize
public spanks, but spanking or criticizing in public
can often be demeaning. I believe we ought to try
as often as possible to spank (i.e., criticize or correct) in private and thank in public as well as in
private. This goes a long way in building bridges. I
hope I built many that day.

Thanksgiving as a Discipline

What would happen if verbalizing our gratitude became a regular discipline for us, even more so than verbalizing our dissent, complaints and displeasure? It is so easy to complain and fight for our rights. It is easy to tell others what they are doing wrong. I know this from personal experience. But guess what? There are a lot of people who are doing things right, and we need to thank them. In so doing, we build bridges with multiple lanes. Lanes of justice and forgiveness are crucial but we often forget to add lanes of gratitude and celebration.

Are You the One?

When was the last time you thanked someone for his or her forgiveness? When was the last time someone extended grace to you? Did you take the grace for granted and move on, or did you pause and say thank you? As elementary as this may sound, Jesus knows that our propensity is to be like the nine thankless lepers who received healing from Christ rather than the one who returned to say thanks (Luke 17:11-19).

The one leper that returned was a Samaritan. Isn't it interesting that Jesus highlights that the foreigner made the effort to show gratitude?

This is instructive for us because I believe that

forgraceness is what brings healing, but gratitude and thanksgiving bring sealing. If you want to seal something of significance, then return to the one who blessed you and say thank you. If you want favor in the future, don't be ungrateful, go back and show gratitude.

If giving thanks didn't matter, Jesus would not have mentioned it. But it mattered to him. Even Jesus likes to hear "Thank you."

Maybe you want to pass this book on to someone who has forgraced you. As a way to say thank you for forgiveness and grace, return a courteous word of thanks to close the loop and seal the act of forgraceness. Going platinum is such a selfless act that at the very least it deserves heartfelt thanks. If this is true, then bless someone with these words: "You have helped me tremendously with your love, your kindness and your grace. Thank you."

9

Keeping an Attitude of Forgraceness

Attitude is our predisposition to act. You can prepare and position yourself to respond to negative things before they happen. Who says we have to react negatively to negativity? We can choose to respond positively to negativity even when our natural bent is to do otherwise. There is a fourfold process to developing this skill.

Pray in the Morning

We must prayerfully prepare ourselves for the possibility of experiencing unscheduled encounters by *praying in the morning*.

Jesus had the ability to know ahead of time what each day would hold. We do not. But we do know who holds our day. God. As long as we connect with him and begin our day by meditating on him, whether we do this before we sleep at night (I realize that nighttime is morning for some) or after we rise in the morning, preparing our spirit positions us to face the unexpected.

I don't think that I have a great prayer life at all, but I can say that I have worked at this for years and have learned that falling on my knees when I get out of the bed for a short prayer has been a helpful way of greeting the Lord and preparing for the day.

Pray in the Moment

Second, remember that we can also *pray in the moment*. When Jesus was being crucified, he prayed for the Father's forgiveness toward his persecutors. We too can pray in the moment and ask God for strength, peace and an eternal perspective, even in excruciating pain.

There have been many times when I have said in the moment, "Lord, please help me not to kill this person!" (Of course, I am using hyperbole.) Just yesterday as my young daughter and I were in traffic, a minivan pulled alongside our car and attempted to butt in. My daughter said to me, "Daddy, is that van in the correct lane?" I responded, "No, she is not. She is trying to butt in by driving in the median portion of the road, and that is against the law."

I had every negative thought going through my head about the driver. Secretly, I had hoped a police officer noticed her transgression. I was tempted to drive forward and not let her in front of me so that she'd be stuck on the median. That's bad, isn't it? I know. Shameful!

In my softer nature (or maybe because of my daughter's presence) and through the presence of the Holy Spirit, I yielded and allowed the driver to get in front of me. She thought she had won and probably surmised that I yielded to her aggressive driving prowess. I knew that I was yielding to the Holy Spirit.

The driver could have at least given a wave of gratitude or acknowledgment, right? Nope! Not even a thank you! I'm glad it was God I was yielding to. Praying in the moment is what made all the difference in my ability to let it go and move on.

Pray in Motion

The third thing that helps us keep a platinum attitude so that we forgrace others is to *pray in motion*. This is the continual act of being prayerfully connected with God. It is the idea of praying without ceasing (1 Thessalonians 5:17).

While you are going through your day at work, school, grocery shopping or doing laundry, staying connected to the presence and power of God is an ongoing conversation. It is like having our computer opened to a prayer file or website, which remains on throughout the day. While we may use various files and websites, we keep the prayer file open on our desktop, interacting with it regularly.

That seems to be what continual prayer is. It is not opening and closing the computer. It is keeping it open, accessible and available as we continually interact, weaving in and out, throughout the day.

Our "amen" at the end of our morning or evening prayer is not shutting down our computer until the next time we pray. Conversely, our "amen" at the end of a prayer is more like minimizing our computer screen for more interaction throughout the day. When we do this, we'll find that we receive ongoing e-mail chimes, Facebook messages and tweets from on high throughout the day. It's akin to being socially networked with God all day long. Prayer is an open and ongoing conversation where we use *amen* as a comma, not a period.

Pray in Mourning

Finally, *pray in mourning*. What I mean is that our grief and pain matters to God. Jesus' grief and pain mattered to God the Father even when Jesus was accomplishing his purpose of atonement for humanity on the cross. When we hurt or experience the injustice of others' bad behavior, forgraceness is the last thing any of us want to offer. It is not easy to walk away from our offenders and let them off the hook.

I am not saying that we don't seek justice. I am saying, however, that our mourning matters to God as much as justice does, and he feels our pain. Leave justice to the authorities and to God, the ultimate authority. Our healing and wholeness will come as we keep a platinum attitude of forgraceness and as we take our mourning to the one who comforts and is close to the brokenhearted. He is the one who will look at us one day, as I'm sure he did when the risen Lord first returned to heaven, and say, "Well done, good and faithful servant."

A Final Thought

Platinum-level living is possible. Forgraceness is the practical way of doing good to those who have hurt you. Forgraceness is God's avenue of redemption in personal relationships and among groups.

There is hope for you, and you have the ability to be a forgracer with God's help. It takes prayer and the power of God's Spirit, but I know you can do it. With God all things are possible. Your freedom awaits you. Let go of the grudge, and live the way God intends. Free in Christ. Free indeed.

An Invitation

Allow me to ask *the* most important question. Have you placed your faith in Jesus Christ? Have you invited his grace and forgiveness into your life? He longs to forgive every sin in your life and promises to wash you clean from your unrighteousness. The process is quite simple. Salvation comes through faith. When we hear the good news that Christ is willing to forgive all of our sins based on his love, all we have to do is respond in faith by accepting the love of Christ.

If you have not responded positively to the love of Christ by inviting him into your life personally, then pause now and sincerely ask God to come into your life. He will begin a new relationship with you if you invite him to do so.

Here is a short prayer you can pray. You can also

use your own words. God wants to hear your heart, and he will answer this prayer:

> Dear God, I recognize my need for your grace and your forgiveness in my life. I am deeply sorry for ignoring or rejecting you. Today I choose to follow you by faith. Help me understand how my wrongdoings and shortcomings have separated me from you.
>
> Please come into my life, my thoughts and my heart. Thank you for taking away the penalty of eternal separation from you for all my errors, faults and sins when you paid the price for my salvation on the cross of crucifixion. May I rise again to new life by your forgiveness and grace, by the same power that caused Jesus to rise again from the dead. I now receive your forgraceness by faith by inviting you to save me from eternal separation from you. Thank you for forgracing me. I receive your gift of salvation now. In Jesus' name, amen.

If you sincerely prayed for Christ to come into your life, the Bible teaches that you now have him in you spiritually, and a new life is being birthed inside of your spirit even as you read this.

Congratulations! Your new life starts now.

(Send me an e-mail me at info@Anderson-

Speaks.com and let me know that you prayed this prayer. I will connect you to some resources that will help you understand how to grow and develop in your new faith journey.)

Maybe you have already placed your faith in Jesus Christ as your Lord and Savior but the difficulties of life have weighed you down, and you too are feeling the burden of unforgiveness and the pressure of gracelessness closing in on you. I pray that today this book will positively change your life as you commit yourself to living a life of forgraceness.

A Gift to Give Away

In a world where precious metals like platinum are worth so much, the platinum rule that you have read about and are contemplating has eternal value that will last forever.

Consider who you might pass this book on to as a gift of ultimate value. Should your recipient receive this gift and apply the forgraceness of Jesus to his or her life, you will have passed on something that will remain for eternity, promising forgiveness, freedom, peace and healing forever.

As you give the book away consider passing it on for one or more of the following reasons:

Categories of Gift Recipient

- I love you dearly.

- You've hurt me deeply.

- I apologize sincerely.

- I'm concerned about you personally.

- You've helped me tremendously (thanks for your forgraceness in my life).

When you give away this book, sign it over to the recipient on the following signature page and disclose the reason you are giving it by checking one or more of the boxes.

Signature Page

To: _____

From: _____

Date: _____

I am giving you this book as a gift because of the box(es) I checked below. I want you to know that I forgrace you. I have recognized my need for forgiveness and grace, and I am convinced that I must extend to you what I have received from God.

☐ I love you dearly.

☐ You've hurt me deeply.

☐ I apologize sincerely.

☐ I'm concerned about you personally.

☐ You've helped me tremendously.

BridgeLeader
B O O K S

BridgeLeader Books are produced through a partnership between InterVarsity Press and BridgeLeader Network, a nonprofit organization that helps churches, colleges, companies and other groups move toward multicultural effectiveness. Addressing such topics as reconciliation, diversity and leadership development, BridgeLeader Books contribute to a better understanding and practice of multicultural ministry within the church and in the world.

For more information about David A. Anderson and Bridgeway Community Church, visit

www.Bridgewayonline.org

www.BridgeLeaderNetwork.com

www.AndersonSpeaks.com

Also by David A. Anderson:

Gracism: The Art of Inclusion

Multicultural Ministry Handbook: Connecting Creatively to a Diverse World, coedited with Margarita R. Cabellon

Both books are available at InterVarsity Press, www .ivpress.com.